MW01593131

Thieves Can't Steal

Our Eternal Treasures

Lillie Rhodes Manley

Printed in the United States of America

First Printing,2018
ISBN-13: 978-1720319061

ISBN-10: 1720319065

David Rhodes Publishing
Treasureify Books
Sweet Whispers of Hope Publishing
190 Blue Goose Rd
Beech Bluff, TN   38313

www.treasureify.com

Disclaimer

Terms of Use

You are given a non-transferable, "personal use" license to this product. You cannot distribute it or share it with other individuals.

Also, there are no resale rights or private label rights granted when purchasing this document. In other words, it's for your own personal use only.

This book is printed on fine modern quality paper. This paper has been specially produced to be acid free (neutral pH) and contains no groundwood or unbleached pulp. It contains with all of the requirements of the American National Standards Institute, Inc., so as to ensure that this book will last and be enjoyed by future generations.

Thieves Can't Steal

Our Eternal Treasures

Table of Contents

This is a book of short devotionals including prose and Scripture verses that are intended to be a reminder to all of us of the grace and mercy of our gracious God.

Foreword

 I read Lillie's poems on Facebook and was happy to receive a copy of her new book, *Thieves Can't Steal Our Eternal Treasures;* the poems are the expression of her deep devotion to our Lord Jesus Christ. They reveal her personal experiences of fellowship with Him through reading the Bible both Old and New Testaments and prayer.

The poems contain teaching from Scripture that is both easy to understand and yet profound. Lillie's poems explain theological terms such as justification, sanctification, and glorification in a way that people who have had little or no teaching can understand. Her understanding of the theological terms is from everyday living that reveals the truths she writes about in the poems. Her poems shine the spotlight on the birth, life, death, and resurrection of our Lord Jesus Christ that make possible our justification, sanctification, and glorification.

Every Christian is called to be and to make disciples. Only a small percentage of Christians will stand before a congregation or small group to teach or make disciples. The greater majority will teach others by obeying the commandments of Jesus. Lillie's poems reveal that she is a disciple and she uses poetry to make disciples of others. Each of Lillie's poems contains three parts: poem, promise, and focus. Her poetry follows the Old Testament poetry pattern which cause the reader to pause and think about what they are reading.

The person who believes on the Lord Jesus Christ to save them from the slavery of sin and death receive the Holy Spirit. The Holy Spirit pours God's love into the heart of the believer (Romans 5:15) that makes it possible to love God and the neighbor (Matthew 22:36-40). Lillie's poems unquietly combine the Holy Spirit, God's love, and love of God and neighbor.

Lillie's poems are written out of inspiration from fellowship with the Father, Son, and Holy Spirit.

The inspiration she receives is conveyed to the reader of the poems. She could have kept the inspiration to herself, but she chose to share it with others. Salvation, fellowship, and inspiration are God's grace to us. God's grace isn't to be received for ourselves but to be shared with others. Lillie's poems are doing that.

Thieves Can't Steal Our Eternal Treasures is written in a way that people who aren't Christians, people who have only been Christians a short period of time, and those who have been Christians for years can all reap benefits from reading it. The book would be ideal to read as a daily devotional. Hopefully you will be as inspired as I was from reading the book.

Robert P. Holland, Pastor, Author, and Discipleship Blogger

Introduction

If, with a repentant heart, we have accepted God's gift of grace, we have a gift that is much more valuable than anything in this world and beyond. It is a gift that no thief can steal.

Through His grace, Jesus went to the cross with every sin of every person of every generation on His shoulders. There He paid the price of every sin; and He did this because of His grace.

Through His grace, our soul receives salvation. Through His grace, we are flooded with His Love and Light, made possible by His precious Holy Spirit.

His Holy Spirit is with us during the good times and as our Comforter, during the hard times.

With His sweet Holy Spirit living inside us we have access to our Teacher, our Comforter, our Advocate, and our Friend. Our Friend, like no other, will lead us safely home where we will be with our Lord and our loved ones forever.

Nothing can compare to this wonderful gift; and no thief can steal this from us.

Having said all of this, we are reminded in the Gospels about two thieves who were being crucified on each side of Jesus. One of them sarcastically cursed our Lord; the other said, "Lord, remember me when You come into Your Kingdom." Jesus assured Him, "Today You will be with Me in Paradise." This is a blessed confirmation that no one is beyond our Lord's redeeming grace.

It is my prayer that you will receive a blessing from the following pages as we share together the blessing that Thieves Can't Steal Our Eternal Treasures.

With much love,
Lillie Manley

In Loving Memory of Jerry Wayne Manley

1/07/1948 – 4/29/2011

A special thank you to all my family and friends. Your love is truly one of my eternal treasures that *Thieves Can't Steal.*

Chapter 1

God's Grace for You

Please bless us with Your grace.
We are so in need of You.
As we pray – Give us faith
 that You will see us through.

God's Promise:
And I am certain that God who began the good work within you will continue His work until it is finally finished on the day when Christ Jesus returns.
Philippians 1: 6

Focus:
God's grace is an undeserved gift.

Thank You, Jesus!

God's greatest gift of love to us
is the grace that He imparts –
It's the precious blood of Calvary
that reaches to our heart.

God's Promise:
I do not treat the grace of God as meaningless. For if keeping the law could make us right with God, then there was no need for Christ to die. Galatians 2: 21

Focus:
Grace does for us what rules and law could not do.

Thank You, Jesus!

The living God is among us.
We can sense Him everywhere.
The God who parted the Red Sea
hears our every prayer.

God's Promise:
Jesus Christ is the same yesterday,
today, and forever.
Hebrews 13: 8

Focus:
Because of His grace, His love will
never change.

Thank You, Jesus!

God's Love is unconditional.
It refreshes us anew.
As we trust His saving grace,
it will flow through me and you.

God's Promise:
We are made right with God by placing our faith in Jesus Christ. This is true for everyone who believes, no matter who we are.
Romans 3: 22

Focus
God's grace is unconditional. It cannot be bought or earned. It is ours to accept as His Own gift.

Thank You, Jesus!

Blessings from Heaven –
Our Lord gives to us.
In good times and hard times –
His grace is enough.

God's Promise:
I know how to live on almost nothing
or with everything.
Philippians 4: 11a

For I can do everything through
Christ who gives me strength.
Philippians 4: 13

Focus:
Jesus is all we need. Lord, we lean
on You.

Thank You, Jesus!

Lord, help us surrender
as we humbly seek Your face.
Let Your Spirit flow through us –
through Your love, and grace.

God's Promise:
If you look for me wholeheartedly,
you will find me.
Jeremiah 29: 13

Focus:
If we seek Him, we will find.

Thank You, Jesus!

Our great God is only reachable
through eyes of trust and faith.
The power of His Presence
overflows our heart with grace.

God's Promise:
We praise God for the glorious grace
He has poured out on us who belong
to His dear Son.
Ephesians 1: 6

Focus:
When we trust Him, He gives His
grace.

Thank You, Jesus!

Sometimes only God can see
the deep wounds of our heart.
Only He can heal the scars,
and grace – to us – impart.

God's Promise:
And I will give you a new heart, and I will put a new spirit within you. I will take out your stony, stubborn heart and give you a tender, responsive heart.
Ezekiel 36: 26

Focus:
Only God can give us a new heart, saturated with His grace.
Thieves can't steal our new heart.

Thank You, Jesus!

The finished work on Calvary
Is our Father's gift to us.
He took our place, amazing grace!
How we praise Him for His love!

God's Promise:
He is so rich in kindness and grace
that He purchased our freedom with
the blood of His Son and forgave our
sins.
Ephesians 1: 7

Focus:
He purchased our freedom through
His great grace.

Thank You, Jesus!

Lord, Your Love – so abundant –
Gives us strength to go on.
Your grace – so sufficient –
Will carry us home.

God's Promise:
"My grace is sufficient for you. My power works best in weakness."
2 Corinthians 12: 9

Focus:
God's grace is sufficient!
He is all we need!

Thank You, Jesus!

We are joint heirs with Jesus!
Our sins are erased!
We'll live forever in glory -
because of His Grace!

God's Promise:
And since we are His children, we are His heirs. In fact, together with Christ we are heirs of God's glory. But if we are to share His glory, we must also share His sufering.
Romans 8: 17

Focus:
Because of His grace, we are heirs of God's glory.

Thank You, Jesus!

We've wandered in the wilderness,
lost, lonely, and afraid.
Our thirst was quenched –
When we drank -
From God's endless well of grace.

God's Promise:
"But those who drink the water I give will never be thirsty again. It becomes a fresh, bubbling spring within them, giving eternal life.
John 4: 14

Focus:
God's grace is our endless well of living water.

Thank You, Jesus!

The simplicity of the Gospel
is Heaven's sweetest song.
Our Father's gift of grace to us
will lead us safely home.

God's Promise:
And He gives grace generously. As the Scriptures say, "God opposes the proud but gives grace to the humble. James 4: 6

Focus:
The simplicity of the Gospel is simply trusting God's grace.

Thank You, Jesus!

God's grace is so amazing –
It is hard to comprehend.
Yet it is so simple –
A child can understand.

God's Promise:
"I tell you the truth, unless you turn from your sins and become like little children, you will never get into the Kingdom of Heaven.
Matthew 18: 3

Focus:
We must become as humble and trusting as a little child.

Thank You, Jesus!

We are God's uncut jewels,
that He is polishing with grace.
He is molding us for heaven –
Where we shall behold His face.

God's Promise:
Dear friends, we are already God's children, but He has not yet shown us what we will be like when Christ appears. But we do know that we will be like Him, for we will see Him as He really is. And all who have this eager expectation will keep themselves pure, just as He is pure.
1 John 3: 2-3

Focus:
Our Lord covers us with grace.

Thank You, Jesus!

As our Protector and Provider,
God walks with us – day by day.
He protects us with His mercy,
and empowers us with grace.

God's Promise:
Don't be afraid, for I am with You.
Don't be discouraged, for I am your
God. I will strengthen you and help
you. I will hold you up with My
victorious right hand.
Isaiah 41: 10

Focus:
Our Lord empowers us with His
grace. He holds us up with His
victorious right hand.

Thank You, Jesus!

He a-rose and He is living!
He is preparing us a place!
Our sins are covered by His blood
through His glorious gift of grace.

God's Promise:
"We believe that we are all saved the same way, by the undeserved grace of the Lord Jesus."
Acts 15:11

Focus:
We are saved by God's amazing grace!

Thank You, Jesus!

What kind of love would say,
"I'll go.
I will take their place.
I'll give My life that they may live."
We praise Him for His grace!

God's Promise:
"Now My soul is deeply troubled. Should I pray, 'Father, save me from this hour'?   But this is the very reason I came, Father. Bring glory to Your Name."
John 12: 27-28

Focus:
Jesus came to earth to take our place on the cross.

Thank You, Jesus!

Upon the shoulders of our Lord,
All our sins were placed.
He bore our shame;
He took our pain -
because of His Amazing Grace!

God's Promise:
Yet it was our weaknesses He carried; it was our sorrows that weighed Him down. And we thought His troubles were a punishment from God, a punishment for His own sins! But He was pierced for our rebellion, crushed for our sins. He was beaten so we could be whole. He was whipped so we could be healed. Isaiah 53: 4-5

Focus:
Our sins carried Him to the cross.

Thank You Jesus!

Before our sins were committed,
By His hand, they were erased.
Washed away with His blood –
From His basin of pure grace.

God's Promise:
He got up from the table, took off His robe, wrapped a towel around His waist, and poured water into a basin. Then He began to wash the feet of His disciples, drying them with the towel.
John 13: 4-5

Focus:
Through His grace, our sins are washed away.

Thank You, Jesus!

When we've feasted at His table,
His grace saturates our soul.
We don't have to fear the dark.
Our Lord is in control!

God's Promise:
Sin is no longer your master, for you no longer live under the requirements of the law. Instead, you live under the freedom of God's grace.
Romans 6: 14

Focus:
We live under the freedom of God's grace.

Thank You, Jesus!

God specializes in mending
Helpless and hopeless hearts.
If we seek Him and believe,
His grace – He will impart.

God's Promise:
He heals the brokenhearted and
bandages their wounds.
Psalm 147: 3

Focus:
Jesus can heal our broken and
Wounded heart.

Thank You, Jesus!

Nothing is quite so wonderful
As God's Spirit – sweet and dear.
Nothing quite so amazing -
as God's grace that holds us near.

God's Promise:
But even greater is God's wonderful grace and His gift of forgiveness to many through Jesus Christ.
Romans 5: 15b

Focus:
God's grace is greater than all our sins.

Thank You, Jesus!

Our Lord chooses to use us,
Although we're so unworthy.
He will do His work through us;
His grace makes us worthy.

God's Promise:
Yet God, in His grace, freely makes
us right in His sight. He did this
through Christ Jesus when He freed
us from the penalty of our sins.
Romans 3: 24

Focus:
In God's grace, we are made
worthy.

Thank You, Jesus!

God's golden thread of forgiveness
From Genesis to Revelation –
Is His glorious gift of grace
that assures our soul salvation.

God's Promise:
If the law could give us new life, we could be made right by obeying it. But the Scriptures declare that we are all prisoners of sin, so we receive God's promise of freedom only by believing in Jesus Christ.
Galations 3: 21b-22

Focus:
God's golden thread of forgiveness is the grace He gives us.

Thank You, Jesus!

Because He lives – we too can live.
We no longer walk alone.
On that day – our debt was paid
by grace – and grace alone.

God's Promise:
For if you are trying to make
yourselves right with God by keeping
the law, you have been cut off from
Christ! You have fallen away from
God's grace.
Galatians 5: 4

Focus:
We are saved by grace and grace
alone!

Thank You, Jesus!

If Jesus wasn't living
In this world we're living in.
Alone we'd grope,
beneath the load
of our burdens, guilt, and sin.

God's Promise:
Then Jesus said, "Come to Me, all of
you who are weary and carry heavy
burdens, and I will give you rest."
Matthew 11: 28

Focus:
Jesus longs to lift the heavy burdens
we are carrying and carry them for
us.

Thank You, Jesus!

Our new life will last forever
because of His eternal grace.
In His grand eternity,
we'll look upon His blessed face.

God's Promise:
Now may our Lord Jesus Christ
Himself and God our Father, who
loved us and by His grace gave us
eternal comfort and wonderful hope,
comfort you and strengthen you in
every good thing you do and say.
2 Thessalonions 2: 6-7

Focus:
His grace is eternal!

Thank You, Jesus!

A place where grief cannot come.
Our tears will be erased.
We'll be with Him forever
through His Amazing Grace!

God's Promise:
For the Lamb on the throne will be
their Shepherd. He will lead them to
springs of life-giving
water. And God will wipe every tear
from their eyes.
Revelation 7: 17

Focus:
We will drink from springs of life-giving
water. And our tears will all
be gone.

Thank You, Jesus!

His wondrous grace – sufficient
floods our weary soul with peace.
Wonderful and amazing!
His grace for you and me!

God's Promise:
Each time He said, "My grace is
sufficient for you. My power shows
up best in weakness."
2 Corinthians 12: 9a

Focus:
God's grace is sufficient in every
circumstance.

Thank You, Jesus!

In God's sea of forgetfulness,
our sins have been erased.
As far as the east is from the west,
He keeps us by His grace.

God's Promise:
He has removed our sins as far from
us as east is from the west.
Psalm 103: 12

Focus:
Just as if we never sinned, our sins
have been removed.
All because of God's Amazing Grace!

Thank You, Jesus!

At God's Throne – grace is found!
Lord – Help us to remember –
That we never walk alone –
To You – Lord – we surrender.

God's Promise:
We can say with confidence,
"The Lord is my helper, so I will have
no fear. What can mere
people do to me.
Hebrews 13:6

Focus:
We never walk alone.

Thank You, Jesus!

Our love for our Lord is greater
than love of worldly gain.
God's gift of grace is greater
than riches or worldly fame.

God's Promise:
But you belong to God, my dear
children. You have already won a
victory over those people, because
the Spirit who lives in you is greater
than the spirit who lives in the
world.
1 John 4: 4

Focus:
God's grace is our greatest treasure.
Thieves cannot steal.

Thank You, Jesus!

Jesus is our tender Shepherd.
Yet He is our coming King.
By grace – we're His forever.
His praise – to Him – we sing.

God's Promise:
They will never again be hungry or thirsty; they will never be scorched by the heat of the sun. For the Lamb on the throne will be their Shepherd.
Revelation 7: 16-17a

Focus:
Because of His grace, the Lamb on the throne is our Shepherd and our coming King.

Thank You, Jesus!

Whatever comes our way – Lord –
May we – Your will – embrace.
Please lead us with Your Spirit
and Your unfolding grace.

God's Promise:
 We don't look at the troubles we can see now;
rather, we fix our gaze on things that cannot be seen. For the things we see now will soon be gone, but the things we cannot see will last forever.
2 Corinthians 4: 17-18

Focus:
God's unfolding grace lets us see through eyes of faith.

Thank You, Jesus!

Our heart can't comprehend
a Father's Love – so great!
What kind of love – would give us
pure mercy – love – and grace!

God's Promise:
God saved us and called us to live a
holy life. He did this, not because we
deserved it, but because that was His
plan from before the beginning of
time – to show us His grace through
Christ Jesus.
2 Timothy 1: 9

Focus:
It is hard to comprehend God's
wonderful gift of grace.

Thank You, Jesus!

God's Light never diminishes!
His power never fades!
Though we may fail and falter,
He holds us with His grace.

God's Promise:
We praise God for the glorious grace
He has poured out on us who belong
to His dear Son.
Ephesians 1: 6

Focus:
He holds us with His grace.

Thank You, Jesus!

Jesus washed the disciples' feet.
He gave His gift of grace.
He knew they would abandon Him;
yet with mercy – He forgave.

God's Promise:
He (Jesus) got up from the table, took off His robe, wrapped a towel around His waist, and poured water into a basin. Then He began to wash the disciples' feet, drying them with the towel He had around Him.
John 13: 4-5

Focus:
He still forgives.

Thank You, Jesus!

His hand set the moon and stars,
formed a human from the dust.
The same hands endured the cross
to give grace to all of us.

God's Promise:
When I look at the night sky and see
the work of Your finges – the moon
and the stars You set in place – what
are mere mortals that You should
think about them, human beings that
You should care for them?
Psalm 8: 3-4

Focus:
The God of the universe loves us.

Thank You, Jesus!

Dear Lord, as lowly children,
we humbly seek Your face.
We know Your touch can fill us
With Your great, infinite grace.

God's Promise:
"Anyone who becomes as
humble as this little child is the
greatest in the Kingdom of
Heaven."
Matthew 18: 4

Focus:
When we humbly seek Him –
We will find.

Thank You, Jesus!

We feel God's Holy Spirit,
like a tender, warm embrace.
We can't earn or deserve it.
It is His gift of grace.

God's Promise:
God saved you by His grace when you believed. And you can't take credit for this; it is a gift from God. Salvation is not a reward for the good things we have done, so none of us can boast about it.
Ephesians 2: 8-9

Focus:
Salvation is God's gift of grace.

Thank You, Jesus!

Through His tender Love –
He offers rest,
as in Him – we abide.
Not by works – lest we should
boast,
But by grace – He has supplied.

God's Promise:
Let us come boldly to the throne of
our gracious God. There we will
receive His mercy, and we will find
grace to help us when we need it
most.
Hebrews 4: 16

Focus:
Our Lord is the supplier of grace.

Thank You, Jesus!

One day we'll see our Savior
and feel His warm embrace.
How can we ever thank Him
for His amazing grace?

God's Promise:
Because of His grace He made us
right in His sight and gave us
confidence that we will inherit
eternal life.
Titus 3: 7

Focus:
We will praise Him eternally for His
glorious gift of grace.

Thank You, Jesus

Our Savior is preparing
a wonderful, perfect place.
We'll receive a great welcome
 because of His grace.

God's Promise:
I have fought the good fight. I have finished the race, and I have remained faithful. And now the prize awaits me – the crown of righteousness, which the Lord, the righteous Judge, will give me on the day of His return. And the prize is not just for me but for all who eagerly look forward to His appearing.
2 Timothy 4: 7-8

Focus:
Our grace is eternal!

Thank You, Jesus!

If our Lord can clothe the lily's
with beauty and grace –
How much more will He clothe us –
when we seek His face.

God's Promise:
"Look at the lily's and how they
grow. They don't work or make their
own clothing, yet Solomon in all his
glory was not dressed as beautifully
as they are. And if God cares so
wonderfully for flowers that are here
today and thrown
into the fire tomorrow, He will
certainly care for you. Why do you
have so little faith?"
Luke 12: 27-28

Focus:
We are adorned in His grace.

Thank You, Jesus!

Jesus knew from the beginning
the death – He'd have to face.
The pain and torture – sacrifice –
would become our gift of grace.

God's Promise:
"Now my soul is deeply troubled.
Should I pray, 'Father, save Me from
this hour'? But this is the very
reason I came! Father bring glory to
Your Name." Then a voice spoke
from Heaven, saying,
"I have already brought glory to My
Name, and I will do so again."
John 12: 27-28

Focus:
Jesus knew the cross was waiting,
but His love for us was greater.

Thank You, Jesus!

We're all invited to His table.
It's free to all who will partake.
Let us lay aside our difference –
and receive His gift of grace.

God's Promise:
And the angel said to me, "Write this: Blessed are those who are invited to the wedding feast of the Lamb." And He added, "These are true words that come from God."
Revelation 19: 9

Focus:
We have all been invited. The choice is ours.

Thank You, Jesus!

Salvation is total surrender
to the One who took our place.
It's not depending on
performance.
It's simply trusting in His grace.

God's Promise:
Let us come boldly to the throne of our gracious God. There we will receive His mercy, and we will find grace to help us when we need it most.
Hebrews 4: 16

Focus:
Salvation is God's gift of grace.

Thank You, Jesus!

Sometimes Satan's strongholds
appear stronger than our faith.
Lord, help us to lean on You
and trust Your stedfast grace.

God's Promise:
The God of peace will soon crush
Satan under your feet. May the grace
of our Lord Jesus be with you.
Romans 16: 20

Focus:
God's grace is greater than Satan's
strongholds.

Thank You, Jesus!

When we fail to understand, Lord,
We will trust Your grace.
When we can't see Your miracles,
We will see through eyes of faith.

God's Promise:
"If God cares so wonderfully for wildflowers that are here today and thrown into the fire tomorrow, He will certainly care for you.
Why do you have so little faith?"
Matthew 6: 30

Focus:
When we can't see, through faith, we believe.

Thank You, Jesus!

Let us sing redemption's story
To the One who took our place.
He gave us victory over sin -
through His Amazing Grace!

God's Promise:
For sin is the sting that results in
death, and the law gives sin its
power. But thank God! He gives us
victory over sin and death through
our Lord Jesus Christ.
1 Corinthians 15: 55

Focus:
We have won the victory
through God's amazing grace.

Thank You, Jesus!

Adam and Eve disobeyed,
bringing shame to Adam's race.
God covered them with animal skins,
symbolizing His gift of grace.

God's Promise:
And the Lord God made clothing
from animal skins for Adam and his
wife.
Genesis 3: 21

Focus:
God covered Adam and Eve with
animal skins; He has covered us with
grace.

Thank You, Jesus!

The rags we were wearing
Have all been replaced.
The Master has clothed us
with His garment of grace!

God's Promise:
We are all infected and impure with
sin. When we display our righteous
deeds, they are nothing but filthy
rags. Like autumn leaves, we wither
and fall, and our sins sweep us away
like the wind.
Isaiah 64: 6

Focus:
Our Lord has clothed us with His
garment of grace.

Thank You, Jesus!

Chapter 2

The Cross

This bloodstained galilean
was recognized by very few.
He became earth's mockery.
He gave Himself for me and you.

God's Promise:
The crowd watched and the leaders
scoffed. "He saved others," they
said, "let Him save Himself if He is
really God's Messiah, the Chosen
One.
Luke 23: 35

Focus:
He was scoffed for you and me.

Thank You, Jesus!

Jesus longs for all to know Him.
And He wills – not one be lost.
He calls us to share with others
the message of the cross.

God's Promise:
"It was also written that this message would be proclaimed in the authority of His Name to all the Nations, beginning in Jerusalem: There is forgiveness of sins for all who repent. You are witnesses of all these things."
Luke 24: 47-48

Focus:
Forgiveness is ours for the asking.

Thank You, Jesus!

Our God, who is all powerful,
is able to set us free.
The blood He shed at Calvary
gives salvation to you and me.

God's Promise:
The God of our ancestors raised
Jesus from the dead after you killed
Him by hanging Him on a cross.
Then God put Him in the place of
honor at His right hand as Prince
and Savior. He did this so the people
of Israel could repent and be
forgiven.
Acts 5: 30-31

Focus:
Our God is able!

Thank You, Jesus!

The precious blood of Calvary
can reach deep inside our soul.
It can cleanse us! It can heal us!
It can wash us – white as snow!

God's Promise:
"Come now, let's settle this," says the Lord. "Though your sins are like scarlet, I will make them white as snow."
Isaiah 1: 18a

Focus:
Just one drop of His blood can make us white as snow.

Thank You, Jesus!

Lord, deepen our understanding
of Your priceless gift of Love.
Your hand extended on the cross
is our salvation – from above.

God's Promise:
He was pierced for our rebellion,
crushed for our sins. He was beaten
so we could be whole. He was
whipped so we could be healed.
Isaiah 53:5

Focus:
He took our place.

Thank You, Jesus.

"**F**ather, please forgive them.
They know not what they do."
He prayed for those who drove the nails.
He intercedes for me and you.

God's Promise:
Jesus said, "Father, forgive them, for they don't know what they are doing." And the soldiers gambled for His clothes by throwing dice.
Luke 23: 24

Focus:
He prayed for thoses who sinned against Him. He prayed for you and me.

Thank You, Jesus!

The precious flow from Calvary
can cleanse your heart and mine.
Just one drop has power enough
to save the soul of all man-kind.

God's Promise:
He is so rich in kindness and grace
that He purchased our freedom with
the blood of His Son and forgave our
sins.
Ephesians 1: 7

Focus:
One drop of His blood on Calvary has
the power to save all of us.

Thank You, Jesus!

As Jesus walked the Judean hills,
talked with His Father up above.
He saw the horror of the cross,
but His heart was stayed on us.

God's Promise:
"I am praying not only for these
disciples but also for all who will
ever believe in Me through their
message."
John 17: 20

Focus:
We were always on His heart.

Thank You, Jesus!

He doesn't offer money,
but His love is enough.
For it led Him to Calvary.
We're made rich through His blood.

God's Promise:
You know the generous grace of our Lord Jesus Christ. Though He was rich, yet for your sakes, He became poor, so that by His poverty He could make you rich.
2 Corinthians 8: 9

Focus:
Our treasure is eternal.

Thank You, Jesus!

Lord, in our own Gethsemane,
we give our heart to You.
In Your Presence we find strength
to adore and honor You.

God's Promise:
An angel from heaven appeared and
strengthened Him.
Luke 22: 43

Focus:
In our own Gethsemene, our Lord
will send angels to strengthen us just
as they strengthened Jesus.

Thank You, Jesus!

The same blood that saved us
is flowing within.
It's springing forth in us –
again and again.

God's Promise:
"Anyone who believes in Me may
come and drink! For the Scriptures
declare, 'Rivers of living water will
flow from his heart.'"
John 7: 38

Focus:
Our Lord's saving grace is also our
sustaining grace.

Thank You, Jesus!

When Jesus said, "It is finished,"
the dark clouds were rolled away.
God's hand pierced the darkness.
Heaven's dawn began to break.

God's Promise:
When Jesus had tasted it, He said,
"It is finished!" Then He bowed His
head and gave up His Spirit.
John 19: 30

Focus:
The finished work on the cross
resulted in our soul's salvation!

Thank You, Jesus!

God's tears mingle with our tears.
It is as if we're "one."
Because of Calvary, we're accepted
by our Savior – God's Holy Son!

God's Promise:
But You, O Lord, are a God of
compassion and mercy, slow to get
angry and filled with unfailing love
and faithfulness.
Psalm 86: 15

Focus:
Because of the cross, we can be "one"
with our God.

Thank You, Jesus!

Our Lord chose His mission
before the world began.
He chose the rugged cross for us.
Our needs – He understands.

God's Promise:
God chose Him as your ransom long
before the world began, but now in
these last days He has been revealed
for your sake.
1 Peter: 1: 20

Focus:
Our Lord chose to be our
Redeemer long before the world
began. We were on His heart.

Thank You, Jesus!

Our righteous God who hated sin
unleashed wrath on His Son.
The spotless Lamb bore our sins,
and paid the price for everyone.

God's Promise:
It was the precious blood of Christ,
the sinless, spotless Lamb of God.
1 Peter 1: 19

Focus:
Although He was sinless, He became
sin for us.

Thank You, Jesus!

God knows the depth of our sin.
He took them to the cross.
There He was slain,
mocked and shamed -
that we might not be lost.

God's Promise:
Christ suffered for our sins once for all time. He never sinned, but He died for sinners to bring you safely home to God. He suffered physical death, but He was raised to life in the Spirit.
1 Peter 3: 18

Focus:
Jesus died and was risen to bring us safely home to God.

Thank You, Jesus!

Satan tries to achieve a stronghold,
telling us we're good enough.
 We fall short and must be washed
in the fount of Jesus' blood.

God's Promise:
For everyone has sinned; we all fall
short of God's glorious standard.
Romans 3: 23

Focus:
We all fall short and must depend on
the blood of Calvary to cleanse us
from our sin.

Thank You, Jesus!

The very core of the Gospel
is the dear, old rugged cross.
The message is the same to all –
There is salvation for the lost.

God's Promise:
The message of the cross is foolish to those who are headed for destruction! But we who are being saved know it is the very power of God.
1 Corinthians 1: 18

Focus:
Because of the old rugged cross, salvation is possible for all – whoever we are.

Thank You Jesus!

An innocent lamb foreshadowed
the sacrifice for sin.
God's Holy Son shed His blood
that we might be born again.

God's Promise:
He was oppressed and treated
harshly, yet He never said a word.
He was led like a lamb to the
slaughter. And as a sheep is silent
before his shearers, He did not open
His mouth.
Isaiah 53: 7

Focus:
An innocent Lamb foreshadowed our
Lord's sacrifice for our sin.

Thank You, Jesus!

With a kiss of betrayal,
our Savior was seized.
Like a lamb to a slaughter,
for you and for me.

God's Promise:
But even as Jesus said this, a crowd
approached, led by Judas, one of the
twelve disciples. Judas walked over
to Jesus to greet Him with a kiss.
Luke 22: 47

Focus:
When we are betrayed by someone
we love, our Lord understands.

Thank You, Jesus.

As foretold in the Scriptures,
He was crucified and killed.
But on the third day – He arose -
acording to the Father's will.

God's Promise:
But the angel said, "Don't be alarmed. You are looking for Jesus of Nazareth, who was crucified. He isn't here! He is risen from the dead! Look, this is where they laid his body.
Mark 16: 6

Focus:
Because death could not hold our Lord, it cannot hold us. We too will rise!

Thank You, Jesus!

The old rugged cross – now empty
is stained with blood of God's Son.
Even the grave has been vacated!
Death cannot hold the Holy One!

God's Promise:
But very early on Sunday morning
the women went to the tomb, taking
the spices they had prepared. They
found that the stone had been rolled
away from the entrance. So they
went in, but they didn't find the body
of the Lord Jesus.
Luke 24: 1-3

Focus:
Death is defeated!

Thank You, Jesus!

There in total darkness,
the Father turned His face away.
But in those lonely hours,
the sin debt was fully paid.

God's Promise:
By this time it was about noon, and darkness fell across the whole land until three o'clock. The light from the sun was gone. And suddenly, the curtain in the sanctuary of the Temple was torn down the middle.
Luke 23: 44-45

Focus:
The Son of God endured the darkness of the cross for us.

Thank You, Jesus!

His mission was completed
when at last – His blood was shed.
And every sin of everyone
was placed upon His head.

God's Promise:
Then Jesus shouted, "Father, I entrust my Spirit into Your hands!" And with these words He breathed His last.
Luke 23: 46

Focus:
He completed His mission because of His love for us.

Thank You, Jesus!

On an old cross -He suffered.
Because of our sin, He died.
On that day, our Savior made
the ultimate sacrifice.

God's Promise:
I passed on to you what was most
important and what had also been
passed on to me. Christ died for our
sins, just as the Scriptures said.
1 Corinthians 15: 3

Focus:
We can't say it enough. Christ died
for our sins!

Thank You, Jesus!

It matters not how good we are;
we're not quite good enough.
It matters not how bad we are,
He can cleanse us with His blood.

God's Promise:
As a result, no one can ever boast in
the Presence of God. God has united
you with Christ Jesus. For our
benefit God made Him to be wisdom
itself. Christ made us right with
God; He made us pure and holy, and
He freed us from sin. Therefore, as
the Scriptures say, "If you want to
boast, boast only about the Lord.
1 Corinthians 1: 29-31

Focus:
We can boast only of what our Lord
has done.

Thank You, Jesus!

The Son of God – who had no sin became sin for us.
We owed a debt we could not pay.
He paid it with His blood.

God's Promise:
But now you have been united with Christ Jesus. Once you were far away from God, but now you have been brought near to Him through the blood of Christ.
Ephesians 2: 13

Focus:
We have been brought near to God through the blood of Jesus.

Thank You, Jesus!

We're adorned in a spotless robe,
one suitabe for Heaven.
Our robe of flesh is stained in sin.
By His blood – we are forgiven.

God's Promise:
Blessed are those who wash their
robes. They will be permitted to
enter through the gates of the city
and eat the fruit from the tree of life.
Revelation 22: 14

Focus:
Jesus will wash away our sin with
His blood and clothe us in a spotless
robe.

Thank You, Jesus!

The tree of life is ever blooming
in God's heavenly Paradise.
He will give us a grand entrance.
On the cross, He paid our price.

God's Promise:
Then God will give you a grand
entrance into the eternal Kingdom of
our Lord and Savior Jesus Christ.
2 Peter 1: 11

Focus:
Our Lord will personally give us a
grand entrance into our new home.

Thank You, Jesus!

On the Holy Hill of Calvary,
The Lamb of God was slain.
The sacrifice of His Own blood
still covers sin's bright stain.

God's Promise:
But the blood on your door post will serve as a sign, marking the houses where you are staying. When I see the blood, I will pass over you.
Exodus 12: 13a

Focus:
Just as the blood on the door posts covered the Hebrew children, the blood that Jesus shed on Calvary covers our soul.

Thank You, Jesus!

The blood can wash each soul,
though it's trampled on by men.
It cleanses each repentant heart
And blots out every sin.

God's Promise:
For I am not ashamed of this good news about Christ. It is the power of God at work, saving everyone who believes.
Romans 1:16a

Focus:
The blood of Jesus will never lose its power.

Thank You, Jesus!

We don't trust in self-salvation.
for without Him – we'd be lost.
Our heart finds sweet salvation
through the crimson of the cross.

God's Promise:
As for me, may I never boast about anything except the cross of our Lord Jesus Christ. Because of that cross, my interest in this world has been crucified, and the world's interest in me has also died.
Galations 6: 14

Focus:
We cannot boast about anything except the cross.

Thank You, Jesus

Our Lord is sending out a plea;
for He wills – not one be lost.
His heart is breaking as He calls,
"There is salvation at the cross."

God's Promise:
"Look! I stand at the door and knock. If you hear my voice and open the door, I will come in, and we will share a meal together as friends."
Revelation 3: 20

Focus:
The invitation is not for a select few. Jesus carried all our sins to the cross.

Thank You, Jesus!

We become holy by the blood
our Lord shed on the cross.
Through His love for all of us,
He paid the bitter cost.

God's Promise:
God the Father knew you and chose
you long ago, and His Spirit has
made you holy. As a result, you have
obeyed Him and have been cleansed
by the blood of
Jesus Christ.
1 Peter 1: 2

Focus:
Because He is Holy, we too become
holy.

Thank You, Jesus!

Only through the rugged cross
can we enter in.
Jesus is the only One
to grant us pardon for our sin.

God's Promise:
Jesus told him, "I am the way, the
truth, and the life. No one can come
to the Father except through Me."
John 14: 6

Focus:
Jesus is the way, the truth, and the
life.

Thank You, Jesus!

There are no works that we can do
that are quite good enough.
But we can go to Heaven
Only by His blood.

God's Promise:
And this is the way to have eternal
life – to know You, the only true God,
and Jesus Christ, the One You sent to
earth.
John 17: 3

Focus:
Jesus is the only way to live
eternally with Him in Heaven.

Thank You, Jesus!

He was acquainted with our griefs.
Our pain – He understands.
His love for us was on His heart,
as spikes were driven in His hands.

God's Promise:
He was despised and rejected – a man of sorrows, acquainted with deepest grief. We turned our backs on Him and looked the other way. He was despised, and we did not care.
Isaiah 53: 3

Focus:
Jesus can identify with our pain and sorrows because He suffered the pain and rejection of the cross.

Thank You, Jesus!

Lord, in this world of hatred,
please give us faith to stand.
May we know the cross is greater
Than Satan's evil plan.

God's Promise:
Because of our faith, Christ has
brought us into this place of undeserved privilege where we now
stand, and we confidently and
joyfully look forward to sharing
God's glory.
Romans 5: 2

Focus:
The cross is greater than the evil that
surrounds us.

Thank You, Jesus!

God will go to any length
to save His children.
He sent His Own Son to the cross
that we might be forgiven.

God's Promise:
Jesus told them, "My message is not my own; it comes from God who sent Me."
John 7: 16

Focus:
We cannot imagine the depth of God's love for us. It is beyond all human imagination.

Thank You, Jesus!

The blood He shed on Calvary
is the life-line for our soul.
It sustains us as it cleanses,
giving precious life and hope.

God's Promise:
"Anyone who believes in God's Son
has eternal life. Anyone who doesn't
obey the Son will never experience
eternal life but remains under God's
angry judgment."
John 3: 36

Focus:
The cleansing blood from Calvary is
the life-line for our soul.

Thank You, Jesus!

God couldn't turn His back on us.
That's why He chose the cross.
Angels were waiting to intervene.
But for us – He chose the cross.

God's Promise:
"Don't you realize that I could ask my Father for thousands of angels to protect us, and He would send them instantly?"
Matthew 26: 53

Focus:
Jesus didn't have to face the cross. He chose to - because of His great love for you and me.

Thank You, Jesus!

He died to save the very ones
who led Him to the cross –
because His Father's loving heart
willed not one be lost.

God's Promise:
Jesus said, "Father, forgive them, for they don't know what they are doing." And the soldiers gambled for His clothes by throwing dice.
Luke 23: 34

Focus:
When Jesus prayed, "Father forgive them," He was also praying for me and you.

Thank You, Jesus!

No one took the life of Jesus.
Of His own will, He lay it down.
He became the victim of the cross
to give to us a crown.

God's Promise:
God blesses those who patiently endure testing and temptation. Afterward they will receive the crown of life that God has promised to those who love Him.
James 1: 12

Focus:
Because Jesus chose the cross, we will wear a crown of righteousness.

Thank You, Jesus!

The thief saw pure compassion
in our Lord's tear-filled eyes.
The sweetest words – ever heard -
"You'll be with Me in Paradise."

God's Promise:
And Jesus replied, "I assure you,
today you will be with Me in
Paradise.
Luke 23: 43

Focus:
Jesus still whispers to every re-
pentant heart, "You'll be with Me in
Paradise."

Thank You, Jesus!

"Father, forgive them,"
Jesus spoke from the cross.
Without His forgiveness,
every soul would be lost.

God's Promise:
Jesus said, "Father, forgive them, for they don't know what they are doing."
Luke 23: 24a

Focus:
Without His forgiveness, every soul would be lost. Salvation is in no other.

Thank You, Jesus!

God's Covenant is unchangeable.
Jesus came to save the lost.
His finished work will keep us
through the crimson of the cross.

God's Promise:
After supper He took another cup of
wine and said, "This cup is the new
covenant between God and His
people – an agreement confirmed
with my blood, which is poured out
as a sacrifice for you.
Luke 22:20

Focus:
The new covenant is an agreement
confirmed by the blood of the Lamb.

Thank You, Jesus!

Lord, as You walked to Calvary,
 weighed down with our sin.
You gave Your life on this earth
to give life without end.

God's Promise:
As they led Jesus away, a man named Simon, who was from Cyrene, happened to be coming in from the countryside. The soldiers seized Him and put the cross on Him and made Him carry it behind Jesus.
Luke 23-26

Focus:
It was our sins Jesus carried that we might have eternal life.

Thank You, Jesus!

Chapter 3

God's Love

Our Lord is always speaking;
and if we take the time to hear,
our lives will change forever
as His love draws us near.

God's Promise:
Come close to God and God will
come close to you.   Wash your
hands, you sinners; purify your
hearts for your loyalty is divided
between God and the world.
James 4: 8

Focus:
When we reach out to God, He
reaches out and draws us near.

Thank You, Jesus!

It's hard for us to contain
 all you have for us.
As it bubbles over, Lord,
bless others with Your Love.

God's Promise:
Love does no wrong to others, so
love fulfills the requirements of
God's Law.
Romans 13: 10

Focus:
Lord, fill us to overflowing with Your
love.

Thank You, Jesus!

If we know Jesus as our Savior,
we know truth that sets us free.
If we trust and abide in Him,
He will flow through you and me.

God's Promise:
"Abide in me, and I will abide in you.
For a branch cannot produce fruit if
it is severed from the vine, and you
cannot be fruitful unless you remain
in me."
John 15: 4

Focus:
If we abide in Him, He abides in us.

Thank You, Jesus!

Lord, we come with humble heart.
Please heal us with Your touch.
Give us strength to face each day
And go forward in Your Love.

God's Promise:
"Who touched me?" Jesus asked. Everyone denied it, and Peter said, "Master, this whole crowd is pressing up against You." But Jesus said, "Someone deliberately touched me, for I felt healing power go out from me." When the woman realized that she could not stay hidden, she began to tremble and fell to her knees in front of Him.
Luke 8: 45-47

Focus:
His touch will make us whole!

Thank You, Jesus!

From everlasting to everlasting –
our Lord doesn't change.
In sunshine or shadows,
His love remains.

God's Promise:
Jesus Christ is the same yesterday,
today, and forever.
Hebrews 13: 8

Focus:
Our Lord is the same yesterday,
today, and forever.

Thank You, Jesus!

He came to seek and save the lost.
His Word is tried and true.
All who seek Him – find Him.
There's no exception to the rule.

God's Promise:
"For the Son of Man came to seek
and save those who are lost."
Luke 19: 10

Focus:
If we do not know Him, our Lord is
searching for us.

Thank You, Jesus!

Love is forever!
It never ends!
Our Lord will love us forever –
and ever – Amen!

God's Promise:
Prophecy and speaking in unknown languages and special knowledge will become useless. But love will last forever.
1 Corinthians 13: 8

Focus:
Love will last forever!

Thank You, Jesus!

Though kingdoms may crumble
and language may cease.
Love is a treasure
we'll cherish and keep.

God's Promise:
"As surely as my new heavens and
earth will remain, so will you always
be my people, with a name that will
never disappear," says the Lord.
Isaiah 66: 22

Focus:
God's love is a treasure that is ours
forever.

Thank You, Jesus!

Love sent a Savior,
offering life to us all.
Only love will keep lasting
at the world's final call.

God's Promise:
For we know that when this earthly tent we live in is taken down (that is, when we die and leave this earthly body), we will have a house in heaven, an eternal body made for us by God Himself and not by human hands.
2 Corinthians 5: 1

Focus:
We will have an eternal home not made by human hands.

Thank You, Jesus!

Love spoke the universe
and world into place.
Love hung the moon and stars
and planets in space.

God's Promise:
He existed in the beginning with
God.   God created everything
through Him, and nothing was
created except through Him.
The Word gave life to everything that
was created, and His life brought
light to everyone.
John 1: 2-4

Focus:
Jesus is our Living Word!

Thank You, Jesus!

Though flowers are lovely;
they wither and fade.
Even the twinkling stars
will all pass away.
Love is forever! It never fades!

God's Promise:
The grass withers and the flowers
fade, but the Word of our God stands
forever.
Isaiah 40: 8

Focus:
Though other living things will fade
and pass, the Word of our Lord
stands forever!

Thank You, Jesus!

We get a glimpse with prophecy.
But even that will cease.
When we see Jesus as He is,
our joy will be complete.

God's Promise:
If I had the gift of prophecy, and if I understood all of God's secret plans and possessed all knowledge, and if I had such faith that I could move mountains, but didn't love others, I would be nothing.
1 Corinthians 13: 2

Focus:
Though we possess great gifts, without love, we are nothing.

Thank You, Jesus!

For 40 days, He was tempted –
Left and right – on every hand.
Each temptation – He resisted -
because of love for every man.

God's Promise:
Then Jesus, full of the Holy Spirit, returned from the Jordan River. He was led by the Spirit into the wilderness, where He was tempted by the devil for forty days. Jesus ate nothing all that time and became very hungry.
Luke 4: 1-2

Focus:
Though our Lord was tempted, He never gave in to temptation.

Thank You, Jesus!

From everlasting to everlasting
is God's love for His children.
With open arms – He beckons
"Come to Me and be forgiven."

God's Promise:
"Come to me with your ears wide
open. Listen, and you will find life. I
will make an everlasting covenant
with you. I will give you all the
unfailing love I promised to David."
Isaiah 55: 3

Focus:
Our Lord has made an everlasting
covenant with us. His Word is true
forever.

Thank You, Jesus!

The "weeping prophet," Jeremiah,
Preached God's message of love.
With tears, our Lord whispers
that same message unto us.

God's Promise:
Long ago the Lord said to Israel: "I have loved you, my people, with an everlasting love. With unfailing love I have drawn you to myself.
Jeremiah 31: 3

Focus:
Our Lord loves us with an everlasting love.

Thank You, Jesus!

Lord, we entrust our heart to You;
though sometimes we are broken.
But in our brokenness – we find
Your loving arms are open.

God's Promise:
How precious is Your unfailing Love,
O God! All humanity finds shelter in
the shadow of Your wings.
Psalm 36: 7

Focus:
In our brokenness, we find sweet
shelter in Him.

Thank You, Jesus!

From everlasting to everlasting,
our God is true.
With each new dawn He sends us,
His mercies are new.

God's Promise:
The Lord must wait for you to come
to Him so He can show you his love
and compassion. For the Lord is a
faithful God. Blessed are those who
wait for His help.
Isaiah 30: 18

Focus:
Lord, we will wait on You and Your
perfect timing.

Thank You, Jesus!

The closer we draw to God,
more clearly we see –
His heart of compassion
for you and for me.

God's Promise:
For the law never made anything
perfect. But now we have confidence in a better hope, through
which we draw near to God.
Hebrews 7: 19

Focus:
We serve a compassionate God!

Thank You, Jesus!

God fed the Hebrew children
daily manna from above.
Jesus is our Bread from Heaven,
giving great, eternal love.

God's Promise:
Jesus said, "I tell you the truth,
Moses didn't give you bread from
Heaven. My Father did. And now He
offers you the true Bread from
Heaven."
John 6: 32

Focus:
Jesus is our Bread from Heaven.

Thank You, Jesus!

Jesus heard God's whisper,
"There is no other way."
"Father, not my will – but Thine."
our loving Savior prayed.

God's Promise:
He went on a little farther and bowed
with his face to the ground, praying,
"My Father! If it is possible, let this
cup of suffering be taken away from
me. Yet I want Your will to be done,
not mine."
Matthew 26: 39

Focus:
Jesus prayed, "not my will but Thine
be done." Shouldn't we pray the
same way?

Thank You, Jesus!

What a wonderful promise –
our Lord gives to us.
He'll never leave or forsake us.
We're safe in His Love.

God's Promise:
"Teach these new disciples to obey all the commands I have given you. And be sure of this: I am with you always, even to the end of the age."
Matthew 28: 20

Focus:
Jesus will never forsake us!

Thank You, Jesus!

Satan chides us when we fall,
"You might as well give up."
Our Lord gently whispers,
"I will lift you with my love."

God's Promise:
Stay alert! Watch out for your great enemy, the devil. He prowls around like a roaring lion, looking for someone to devour.
1 Peter 5: 8

Focus:
The devil, our enemy, has been defeated by our Lord.

Thank You, Jesus!

We are Yours, Lord,
Your creation – made of dust.
You breathed breath of life in us –
and indwelt us with Your Love.

God's Promise:
For the Spirit of God has made me.
The breath of the Almighty gives me
life.
Job 33: 4

Focus:
We are indwelt by the Holy One who
gives us life.

Thank You, Jesus!

Chapter 4

His Light

When the darkness has ended,
and we're gathered in the Light.
We'll hear Him say,
"My child, well done."
"Welcome home – eternal life."

God's Promise:
The Master was full of praise. "Well
done, my good and faithful servant.
Matthew 25: 21a

Focus:
The words we long to hear, "Well
done, my child."

Thank You, Jesus!

The more we let His light shine,
the brighter it glows.
The longer we walk with Him,
the sweeter He grows.

God's Promise:
The Word gave life to everything that was created, and His Life brought light to everyone. The Light shines in the darkness, and the darkness can never extinguish it.
1 John 1: 5

Focus:
Jesus is our Light in a darkened world.

Thank You, Jesus!

Open our eyes to Your Holy Truth.
May we never be led astray.
Enlighten our heart with Love.
In Godly wisdom, light our way.

God's Promise:
This is the message we heard from Jesus and now declare to you: God is Light, and there is no darkness in Him at all.
1 John 1: 5

Focus:
When we face darkness, He is our Light.

Thank You, Jesus!

When our darkened heart
finds His Light,
we cannot explain it.
But as His Light within us grows,
we have to proclaim it.

God's Promise:
This One who is life itself was revealed to us, and we have seen Him.
And now we testify and proclaim to
you that He is the One who is eternal
life.   He was with the Father and
then He was revealed to us.
1 John 1: 2

Focus:
As His Light floods our heart, we
have to proclaim it.

Thank You, Jesus!

If we find ourselves in darkness,
we know we're not alone.
His Light gently leads us –
into the lights of home.

God's Promise:
For the law was given through Moses, but God's unfailing love and faithfulness came through
Jesus Christ.
John 1: 17

Focus:
We know we can trust His light to lead us.

Thank You, Jesus!

Jesus sparkles like a flawless gem
in a world that's dark with sin.
His Light will glow through us
if we give our heart to Him.

God's Promise:
Jesus spoke to the people once more and said, "I am the Light of the world. If you follow me, you won't have to walk in darkness, because you will have the Light that leads to life."
John 8: 12

Focus:
Jesus is the Light of the world.

Thank You, Jesus!

"Be still in My Presence,"
Our Lord whispers to our heart.
In darkest night, He is our Light.
From us – He won't depart.

God's Promise:
"Be still and know that I am God! I will be honored by every nation. I will be honored throughout the world."
Psalm 46: 10

Focus:
If we are still in His Presence, we will hear His whispers.

Thank You, Jesus!

When we face the darkness,
Light of faith moves in.
For darkness can't remain in light.
Our Lord's Light lives within.

God's Promise:
For you are all children of the light and of the day; we don't belong to darkness and night.
1 Thessalonians 5: 5

Focus:
We are children of the Light!

Thank You, Jesus!

When we give our heart to Jesus,
His Light will flood our soul.
Our broken heart is transformed
into His likeness – pure as gold.

God's Promise:
The people who sat in darkness have
seen a great light. And for those who
lived in the land where death casts
its shadow, a light has shined.
Matthew 4: 16

Focus:
Our broken heart is transformed
into His likeness.

Thank You, Jesus!

When we walk through the valley,
He is by our side.
When darkness falls around us,
He leads us with His Light.

God's Promise:
Even when I walk through the
darkest valley, I will not be afraid,
for You are close beside me. Your
rod and your staff protect and
comfort me.
Psalm 23: 4

Focus:
We don't have to be afraid of the
dark, for Jesus lights the way for us.

Thank You, Jesus!

When we see Him as He is,
Our hearts become all-knowing.
In His Light, there is no night –
just His glorious countenance
glowing.

God's Promise:
And there will be no night there – no
need for lamps or sun – for the Lord
God will shine on them. And they
will reign forever and ever.
Revelation 22: 5

Focus:
We will reign forever with Jesus.

Thank You, Jesus!

In dark of night, He gives Light.
We walk toward Heavens' dawn.
With Him – we'll live eternally
in our glorious, heavenly home.

God's Promise:
For God, who said, "Let there be light in the darkness," has made this light shine in our hearts so we could know the glory of God that is seen in the face of Jesus Christ.
2 Corinthians 4: 6

Focus:
Through knowing Jesus, we can know the glory of God.

Thank You, Jesus!

The beautiful Star of Bethlehem
is the Savior born that day.
He's sending out His lovely glow
to us – to light our way.

God's Promise:
Whatever is good and perfect is a gift
coming down to us from God our
Father, who created all the lights in
the heavens. He never changes or
casts a shifting
shadow.
James 1: 17

Focus:
Jesus is our Shining Star!

Thank You, Jesus!

In His Light, there is great hope
that Heaven is our home.
A place our Lord has prepared,
where our loved ones have gone.

God's Promise:
And His Name will be the Hope of
all the world.
Matthew 12: 21

Focus:
Jesus is the hope of the world.

Thank You, Jesus!

To all of us who will receive,
He has become a precious pearl,
a Light shining in the darkness.
The Savior of the world.

God's Promise:
And now He has made this plain to us by the appearing of Christ Jesus, our Savior. He broke the power of death and illuminated the way to life and immortality through the good news.
2 Timothy 1: 10

Focus:
Jesus illuminated the path that leads to eternal life.

Thank You, Jesus!

Lord, in a world of darkness,
fill our soul with Light.
Through us – Lord – lead others
to find Your glorious Light.

God's Promise:
Jesus spoke to the people once more
and said, "I am the Light of the
world. If you follow me, you won't
have to walk in darkness, because
you will have the Light that leads to
life."
John 8: 12

Focus:
We have the Light that leads to life.

Thank You, Jesus!

Lord, let us be salt and light
in a world that's dark with sin.
We know it must begin with us.
Please light our soul within.

God's Promise:
"You are the salt of the earth. But what good is salt if it has lost its flavor?
Matthew 5:13a

"You are the light of the world – like a city on a hilltop that cannot be hidden.
Matthew 5: 14

Make us salt and light, Lord.

Thank You, Jesus!

Lord, our life is not our own.
We're purchased with a price.
May we be Your reflection –
as we behold Your Light.

God's Promise:
Now we see things imperfectly, like puzzling reflections in a mirror, but then we will see everything with perfect clarity. All that I know now is partial and incomplete, but then I will know everything completely, just as God now knows me completely.
1 Corinthians 13: 12

Focus:
We are God's reflection.

Thank You, Jesus!

When the darkness around us
draws us to our knees,
His Light shines in the darkness,
and fills our soul with peace.

God's Promise:
It is also new. Jesus lived the truth
of this commandment, and you also
are living it. For the darkness is
disappearing, and the true Light is
already shining.
1 John 2: 8

Focus:
God's Light shines through the
darkness of sin.

Thank You, Jesus!

When storms of doubt gather,
and clouds block our view,
Our Lord will part the clouds.
and light comes shining through.

God's Promise:
As a result, you can show others the goodness of God, for He called you out of the darkness into His wonderful Light.
1 Peter 2: 9b

Focus:
Our Lord will part the clouds of darkness.

Thank You, Jesus!

There is no room for compromise.
God's Word stands on its own.
It is the Light that leads our way,
and will one day – lead us home.

God's Promise:
They do not compromise with evil,
and they walk only in His paths.
Psalm 119: 3

Focus:
We cannot compromise with evil.
God's Word stands on its own.

Thank You, Jesus!

When our heart finds His Light,
we cannot explain it.
As His Light grows brighter,
we must proclaim it.

God's Promise:
He does this to make the riches of
His glory shine even brighter on
those to whom He shows mercy, who
were prepared in advance for glory.
Romans 9: 23

Focus:
We must proclaim the Light of His
Love!

Thank You, Jesus!

Living obediently to our Lord
is service unto Him.
Lord, hold us in Your hand,
that your Light will not grow dim.

God's Promise:
"They will be my people," says the
Lord of Heaven's armies. "On that
day when I act in judgment, they will
be my own special treasure. I will
spare them as a father spares an
obedient child."
Malachi 3: 17

Focus:
Our Father holds us as a father holds
his obedient child.

Thank You, Jesus!

Lord, please store Your riches
in hearts of those who love you.
To be a lighthouse on the shore –
To hold nothing else above You.

God's Promise:
No one lights a lamp and then puts it
under a basket. Instead, a lamp is
placed on a stand, where it gives
light to everyone in the house.
Matthew 5: 15

Focus:
Lord, please shine through us.

Thank You, Jesus!

Whatever our hands find to do,
we do with all our might.
God calls us – wherever we are,
to emulate His Light.

God's Promise:
Your eye is like a lamp that provides light for your body. When your eye is healthy, your whole body is filled with light.
Matthew 6: 22

Focus:
We are called to emulate His Light.

Thank You, Jesus!

As Moses' countenance glowed
with God's glorious Light -
May we reflect His glory
every moment of our life.

God's Promise:
When Moses came down Mount
Sinai carrying the two stone tablets
inscribed with the terms of the
covenant, he wasn't aware that his
face had become radiant because he
had spoken to the Lord.
Exodus 34: 29

Focus:
When we spend time with God, our
lives reflect His radiance.

Thank You, Jesus!

God's brilliant Light – on the road
brought Saul to his knees.
Saul's life was changed forever.
When he arose – he could not see.

God's Promise:
As I was on the road, approaching
Damascus about noon, a very bright
light from heaven suddenly shone
down around me.
Acts 22: 6

Focus:
Jesus is the Light!

Thank You, Jesus!

So many souls are unaware
of God's Power to save.
May God's Light shine through us,
and illuminate their way.

God's Promise:
And now He has made all of this
plain to us by the appearing of Christ
Jesus, our Savior. He broke the
power of death and illuminated the
way to life and immortality through
the Good News.
2 Timothy 1: 10

Focus:
Through God's Power, we can illuminate the way for others.

Thank You, Jesus!

With darkness all around us,
His Light shines in our soul.
It's the Light of God's Own Spirit,
giving comfort, peace, and hope.

God's Promise:
Light shines on the Godly, and joy on
those whose hearts are right.
Psalm 97: 11

Focus:
God's Light shines in our soul.

Thank You, Jesus!

When rain became a mighty flood,
Noah was protected by the ark.
When we are blinded by life's rain,
God protects us in the dark.

God's Promise:
But God remembered Noah and all the wild animals and livestock with him in the boat. He sent a wind to blow across the earth, and the floodwates began to recede.
Genesis 8: 1

Focus:
God's Light protects us in the dark.

Thank You, Jesus!

Chapter 5

His Salvation

It's time to recognize His Presence
as He does His work through us.
It's time to share salvation's story
as He leads us with His Love.

God's Promise:
The Lord is my light and my salvation, so why should I be afraid?
The Lord is my fortress, protecting me from danger, so why should I tremble?
Psalm 27: 1

Focus:
It's time for us to share our salvation's story.

Thank You, Jesus!

We build on the strong foundation
of Jesus, God's only Son.
This is the Rock that cannot fail.
The victory is already won.

God's Promise:
The Lord lives! Praise to my Rock!
May the God of my salvation be
exalted!
Psalm 18: 46

Focus:
Jesus is the Rock that cannot fail!

Thank You, Jesus!

Our God cannot be limited
to any one denomination.
When we argue foolishly,
it undermines His great salvation.

God's Promise:
For God is not a God of disorder but
of peace, as in all the meetings of
God's holy people.
1 Corinthians 14: 33

Focus:
Our God is a God of peace.

Thank You, Jesus!

We come with heavy burdens,
and lay them at Your feet.
We know that You will carry them.
Our soul finds sweet relief.

God's Promise:
Give your burdens to the Lord, and
He will take care of you. He will not
permit the godly to slip and fall.
Psalm 55: 22

Focus:
He carries our burdens.

Thank You, Jesus!

Dear Lord – create in us
a heart that's good and pure.
Conform, remake, and mold us
until we have a heart like Yours.

God's Promise:
God blesses those whose hearts are
pure, for they will see God.
Matthew 5: 8

Focus:
Lord, give us a heart like Yours.

Thank You, Jesus!

"**W**hosoever will – may come."
That's our Lord's invitation.
If we believe – we shall receive
God's great gift of salvation.

God's Promise:
The Spirit and the bride say, "Come."
Let anyone who hears this say,
"Come." Let anyone who is thirsty
come. Let anyone who desires drink
freely from the water of life.
Revelation 22: 17

Focus:
Whosoever will – may come.

Thank You, Jesus!

Our works won't win God's Love.
He loves us as we are.
He begins to mold and shape us,
to give us a new heart.

God's Promise:
The reward for trusting Him will be
the salvation of your souls.
1 Peter 1: 9

Focus:
Jesus loves us as we are, then He
begins to mold us into what He
knows we can be.

Thank You, Jesus!

Salvation is knowing Jesus.
His blood is redemption of sin.
It's trusting Him completely
on a journey that never ends.

God's Promise:
For the grace of God has been revealed, bringing salvation to all
people.
Titus 2: 11

Focus:
Our journey with Jesus never ends.

Thank You, Jesus!

Our Great God so loved creation
that He gave His only Son –
to pay the price for our salvation,
giving hope to everyone.

God's Promise:
"For this is how God loved the world:
He gave His One and Only Son, so
that everyone who believes in Him
will not perish but have eternal life.
John 3: 16

Focus:
Jesus paid the price for our salvation.

Thank You, Jesus!

Newborn souls are born of heaven
not by anything on earth.
If we give our heart to Jesus,
He gives us a brandnew birth.

God's Promise:
For you have been born again, but
not to a life that will quickly end.
Your new life will last forever
because it comes from the eternal,
living Word of God.
1 Peter 1: 23

Focus:
We have been born again.

Thank You, Jesus!

He came to redeem His creation
of sin that corrupted the earth.
Our sin was on His shoulders,
as He destroyed Satan's curse.

God's Promise:
"Praise the Lord, the God of Israel,
because He has visited and redeemed His people."
Luke 1: 68

Focus:
He has redeemed us!

Thank You, Jesus!

In our rags of commonness,
how could Jesus love us?
We are His prized possessions.
He holds nothing else above us.

God's Promise:
We are all infected and impure with sin. When we display our righteous deeds, they are nothing but filthy rags.
Isaiah 64: 6a

Focus:
We are God's prized possessions.

Thank You, Jesus!

Lord, we marvel at the promise
You have made to each of us.
The promise of redemption
through Your glorious gift of love.

God's Promise:
He is so rich in kindness and grace
that He purchased our freedom with
the blood of His Son and forgave our
sins.
Ephesians 1: 7

Focus:
We are redeemed through His blood.

Thank You, Jesus!

No moment is quite so great
as our soul's salvation.
Our name written in God's Book
triggers Heaven's celebration.

God's Promise:
All who are victorious will be clothed
in white. I will never erase their
names from the Book of Life, but I
will announce before my Father and
His angels that they are mine.
Revelation 3: 5

Focus:
Our name will never be erased from
the Book of Life.

Thank You, Jesus!

Somewhere between reading Scriptures - of our Father up above - and saying, "Jesus, save me," He washed me in His blood.

God's Promise:
He is so rich in kindness and grace that He purchased our freedom with the blood of His Son and forgave our sins.
Ephesians 1: 7

Focus:
We are washed in the blood of the Lamb.

Thank You, Jesus!

All of heaven is rejoicing
when one lost soul is changed.
When evil is defeated,
and salvation for one is gained.

God's Promise:
"In the same way, there is joy in the
presence of God's angels when even
one sinner repents."
Luke 15: 10

Focus:
There is joy in the presence of God's
angels when one soul is saved.

Thank You, Jesus!

We have found the miracle.
Our hearts have found rebirth.
Lord, hold us gently in Your arms,
and through us – do Your work.

God's Promise:
All praise to God, the Father of our Lord Jesus Christ. It is by His great mercy that we have been born again, because God raised Jesus Christ from the dead. Now we live with great expectation.
1 Peter 1: 3

Focus:
Rebirth is a miracle that thieves can't steal!

Thank You, Jesus!

Lord, we come with humble heart.
Please free our heart of pride.
Give us a heart of a servant, Lord,
with a spirit that's contrite.

God's Promise:
"I restore the crushed spirit of the
humble and revive the courage of
those with repentant hearts."
Isaiah 57: 15b

Focus:
Our Lord will give us a humble heart
like His Own.

Thank You, Jesus!

Dear Lord, we trust in You alone.
for only You are able.
You understand our deepest pain.
You are our only Savior.

God's Promise:
He has sent us a mighty Savior from
the royal line of His servant David.
Luke 1: 69

Focus:
He has sent us a mighty Savior.

Thank You, Jesus!

We can't earn or buy salvation;
for it's by His blood alone.
We must realize our need for Him,
to become His very Own.

God's Promise:
There is salvation in no one else!
God has given no other name under
heaven by which we must be saved.
Acts 4: 12

Focus:
There is salvation in no one
But Jesus.

Thank You, Jesus!

Thank You for Your Master Plan,
the gift of Your salvation.
For the gift of our heavenly home,
with You as our foundation.

God's Promise:
It is like a person who digs deep and
lays the foundation on solid rock.
When the floodwaters rise and break
against that house, it stands firm
because it is well built.
Luke 6: 48

Focus:
Jesus is our foundation.

Thank You, Jesus!

We know our Redeemer lives!
He is the Holy Word!
Every knee will bow one day,
when He stands upon the earth.

God's Promise:
That at the Name of Jesus every knee
should bow, in heaven and
on earth and under the earth.
Philippians 2: 10

Focus:
Every knee will bow one day at the
mere mention of His Name,
"Jesus."

Thank You, Jesus!

Lord, our salvation wasn't cheap;
yet You paid the bitter price.
You bore the pain for all our sin –
to give to us – eternal life.

God's Promise:
For God bought you with a high
price.   You must honor God with
your body.
1 Corinthians 6: 20

Focus:
Jesus paid the price for
Salvation.

Thank You, Jesus!

"Let me lead you to the altar,"
our Lord gently calls.
"The table's spread with
My forgiveness.
The invitation is to all."

God's Promise:
You prepare a feast for me in the presence of my enemies. You honor me by anointing my head with oil. My cup overflows with blessings.
Psalm 23: 5

Focus:
Our cup overflows with His forgiveness.

Thank You, Jesus!

Our goodness is insufficient.
We are covered in sinful mud.
Self-righteousness adds more sin.
We must be washed in the blood.

God's Promise:
Just think how much more the blood of Christ will purify our consciences from sinful deeds so that we can worship the living God. For by the power of the eternal Spirit, Christ offered Himself to God as a perfect sacrifice for our sins.
Hebrews 9: 14

Focus:
We can be washed clean in the blood.

Thank You, Jesus!

The Holy, spotless Lamb of God
can take our sin away.
We're not too good -
We're not too bad –
to kneel and humbly pray.

God's Promise:
It was the precious blood of Christ,
the sinless, spotless Lamb of God.
1 Peter 1: 19

Focus:
We are not too good or too bad to
kneel and pray for forgiveness.

Thank You, Jesus!

Salvation is nothing we do.
It's what our Lord does for us.
He paid the price –
for our eternal life -
when He washed us in His blood.

God's Promise:
But now you have been united with Christ Jesus. Once you were far away from God, but now you have been brought near to Him through the blood of Christ.
Ephesians 2: 13

Focus:
Our Lord paid the price!

Thank You, Jesus!

It becomes difficult to remember
the persons we used to be,
since Jesus set up residence
in our heart – and set us free.

God's Promise:
All of us who have had that veil
removed can see and reflect the glory
of the Lord. And the Lord – who is
the Spirit – makes us more and more
like Him as we are changed into His
glorious Image.
2 Corinthians 3: 18

Focus:
When we give our lives to Jesus, we
are changed.

Thank You, Jesus!

Lord, we await Your coming
with great anticipation.
While we're here, help us share
Your great gift of salvation.

God's Promise:
"You, too, must keep watch! For you
don't know what day Your Lord is
coming."
Matthew 24: 42

Focus:
Lord, help us to share Your
Great Salvation.

Thank You, Jesus!

We're in the world –
Not of the world –
for we have been redeemed.
Our soul, made dirty by our sin,
by Him, has been made clean.

God's Promise:
Don't copy the behavior and customs of this world, but let God transform you into a new person by changing the way you think. Then you will learn to know God's will for you, which is good and pleasing, and perfect.
Romans 12: 2

Focus:
We are in the world – but not of the world.

Thank You, Jesus.

When we give our heart to Him,
our sins are all forgiven.
He changes our direction
to the road that leads to Heaven.

God's Promise:
Trust in the Lord with all your heart;
do not depend on your own
understanding. Seek His will in all
you do, and He will show you which
path to take.
Proverbs 3: 5-6

Focus:
If we trust Him, He will lead us in the
right direction.

Thank You, Jesus!

When we surrender to our Lord,
He saves us from our sin.
There is no room for worldliness,
when He comes to dwell within.

God's Promise:
Let us go right into the Presence of God with sincere hearts fully trusting Him. For our guilty consciences have been sprinkled with Christ's blood to make us clean, and our bodies have been washed with pure water.
Hebrews 10: 22

Focus:
Christ's blood makes us clean.

Thank You, Jesus!

God's transforming miracle
saves our soul from sin.
He begins to mold and shape us
when we are born again.

God's Promise:
Don't be surprised when I say,
"you must be born again."
John 3: 7

Focus:
God begins transforming us when we
are born again.

Thank You, Jesus!

Chapter 6

The Holy Spirit

Lord, thank You for the fountain -
springing up within.
quenching the thirst of our soul,
warming our heart as a friend.

God's Promise:
As the deer longs for streams of
water, so I long for You, O God. I
thirst for God, the living God.
Psalm 42: 1-2

Focus:
Our God quenches our thirst for
Him.

Thank You, Jesus!

We invite You, Holy Spirit.
Please come and take control.
With our heart we worship You.
Lead us where You'd have us go.

God's Promise:
I pray that God, the source of hope, will fill you completely with joy and peace because you trust in Him. Then you will overflow with confident hope through the Power of The Holy Spirit.
Romans 15: 13

Focus:
The Holy Spirit is our confident hope.

Thank You, Jesus!

'Not by force nor by strength,
but by My Spirit,'
says the Lord of Hosts.
His Spirit will empower us,
and lead us as we go.

God's Promise:
It is not by force nor by strength, but by My Spirit, says the Lord of Heaven's Armies.
Zechariah 4: 6

Focus:
His Spirit will empower us.

Thank You, Jesus!

Lord, may we always treasure
Your Spirit that lives within.
May we never squander it –
or give way to the yoke of sin.

God's Promise:
"For My yoke is easy to bear, and the
burden I give you is light."
Matthew 11: 30

Focus:
As we surrender our burdens to
Him, they become light.

Thank You, Jesus!

There is a well of living water –
that is springing up within.
It's the precious Holy Spirit –
that frees us from our sin.

God's Promise:
"Anyone who believes in Me may
come and drink! For the Scriptures
declare,'Rivers of living water will
flow from his heart.'"
John 7: 38

Focus:
The Holy Spirit is like "Rivers of
Living Water."

Thank You, Jesus!

You have made us free,
and Your Spirit lives within.
May we not get entangled
in the yoke of bondage again.

God's Promise:
Don't you realize that all of you
together are the temple of God and
that the Holy Spirit of God lives in
you?
1 Corinthians 3: 16

Focus:
God's Holy Spirit lives in us!

Thank You, Jesus!

The King of the Universe
has called us His friend.
Our grand inheritance
is life without end.

God's Promise:
Remember that the Lord will give
you an inheritance as your reward,
and that the Master we are serving is
Christ.
Colossians 3: 24

Focus:
We are serving Christ in all that we
do.

Thank You, Jesus!

May we not grieve Your Spirit.
For He is You – inside our soul.
May we follow where you lead.
We ask You to take control.

God's Promise:
Do not bring sorrow to God's Holy Spirit by the way you live. Remember, He has identified you as His Own, guaranteeing that you will be saved on the day of redemption.
Ephesians 4: 30

Focus:
May we not grieve God's Holy Spirit.

Thank You, Jesus!

May Your Holy Spirit
be an ever-increasing flow.
May we be open to receive You –
as You infill our heart and soul.

God's Promise:
I say, let the Holy Spirit guide your
lives. Then you won't be doing what
your sinful nature craves.
Galations 5: 16

Focus:
May we be open to Your Spirit, Lord.

Thank You, Jesus!

We are God's masterpiece.
He made our heart His home.
His oil of joy and gladness
becomes our very own.

God's Promise:
Through the Power of the Holy Spirit
who lives within us, carefully guard
the precious truth that has been
entrusted to you.
2 Timothy 1: 14

Focus:
His oil of joy and gladness becomes
our own.

Thank You, Jesus!

When we're in Your Presence,
praying for those so dear,
Your Spirit washes over us –
sometimes moving us to tears.

God's Promise:
The Holy Spirit helps us in our
weakness. For example, we don't
know what God wants us to pray for.
But the Holy Spirit prays for us with
groanings that cannot be expressed
in words.
Romans 8: 26

Focus:
God's Holy Spirit helps us to know
what to pray for.

Thank You, Jesus!

As we focus on God's Presence,
His Spirit draws us to our knees.
With humility and faith,
we find His sweet peace.

God's Promise:
Then you will experience God's peace, which exceeds anything that we can understand. His peace will guard your hearts and minds as you live in Christ Jesus.
Philippians 4: 7

Focus:
His peace exceeds our understanding.

Thank You, Jesus!

When we come to Jesus,
we know God's gift of Love.
And His sweet Holy Spirit
is living in us.

God's Promise:
At the same time Jesus was filled
with the joy of the Holy Spirit, and
He said, "O Father, Lord of heaven
and earth, thank You for hiding
these things from those who think
themselves wise and clever, and for
revealing them to the childlike. Yes,
Father, it pleased You to do it this
way."
Luke 10: 21

Focus:
We must be trusting as a child.

Thank You, Jesus!

Jesus left us with a gift;
peace of heart and mind.
His Holy Spirit indwells us –
abutting space and time.

God's Promise:
"I am leaving you with a gift – peace
of mind and heart. And the peace I
give is a gift the world cannot give.
Don't be troubled or afraid."
John 14: 27

Focus:
He gives us the gift of peace in all
circumstances.

Thank You, Jesus!

As we trust the Words of Jesus,
He helps us understand.
He seals us with His Spirit.
No one can take us from His hand.

God's Promise:
"I give them eternal life, and they will never perish. No one can snatch them away from me."
John 10: 28

Focus:
We are sealed with His Spirit. No one can take us from His hand.

Thank You, Jesus!

In trials – we don't panic.
In our Lord – we simply trust.
In His mercy – He has given
His sweet Spirit unto us.

God's Promise:
So you see, the Lord knows how to
rescue godly people from their trials,
even while keeping the wicked under
punishment until the day of final
judgment.
2 Peter 2: 9

Focus:
We simply trust in our Lord.

Thank You, Jesus!

The sweetest fellowship in life
is that unbroken chord.
It is the precious ties that bind,
while abiding in our Lord.

God's Promise:
Above all, clothe yourselves with
love, which binds us all together in
perfect harmony.
Colossians 3: 14

Focus:
Love binds us together.

Thank You, Jesus!

May we not grieve Your Spirit
with careless thoughts and words.
In Your Power – work through us,
that Your message may be heard.

God's Promise:
Do not bring sorrow to God's Holy
Spirit by the way you live. Re-
member, He has identified you as
His Own, guaranteeing that you will
be saved on the day of redemption.
Ephesians 4: 30

Focus:
May we not grieve Your Spirit, Lord.

Thank You, Jesus!

God promised to send His Spirit.
And to forgive our unbelief.
He is the One who dwells within,
And comforts when we grieve.

God's Promise:
"I will send the Holy Spirit, just as my Father promised."
Luke 24: 49a

Focus:
The Holy Spirit is our Comforter.

Thank You, Jesus!

Jesus let Thomas feel His wounds.
He'll do the same for us.
We may not feel the nail scars.
But we can surely feel His touch.

God's Promise:
Then He said to Thomas, "Put your finger here, and look at my hands. Put your hand into the wound in my side. Don't be faithless any longer. Believe!
John 20: 27

Focus:
We too can feel His touch.

Thank You, Jesus!

May we recognize His voice,
hear His whispers deep within.
May He do His work through us
as our Savior, Lord, and Friend.

God's Promise:
After the earthquake there was a
fire, but the Lord was not in the fire.
And after the fire there was the
sound of a gentle whisper.
1 Kings 19: 12b

Focus:
If we listen for His whispers, we will
hear.

Thank You, Jesus!

He promised not to leave us
to be like orphans in the night.
He sent His Holy Spirit
to be our comfort and our guide.

God's Promise:
"No, I will not abandon you as
orphans – I will come to you."
John 14: 18

Focus:
He would not abandon us as orphans. He sent His dear Holy Spirit.

Thank You, Jesus!

Lord, when we try to pray,
and we can't seem to start.
When the words won't come,
please listen to our heart.

God's Promise:
Guard your heart above all else for it
determines the course of your life.
Proverbs 4: 23

Focus:
He listens to our heart.

Thank You, Jesus!

Our Lord, who is our Comforter,
is residing deep within.
With Love, He shares our sorrow,
gives us strength to smile again.

God's Promise:
Then you will experience God's peace, which exceeds anything we can understand. His peace will guard your hearts and minds as you live in Christ Jesus.
Philippians 4: 7

Focus:
Our Lord is our Comforter.

Thank You, Jesus!

Our Lord has left us with a gift,
of peace of heart and mind.
His Spirit dwells within –
beyond all space and time.

God's Promise:
I am leaving you with a gift – peace of mind and heart. And the peace I give is a gift the world cannot give. So don't be troubled or afraid.
John 14: 27

Focus:
God's gift of peace is one like the world cannot give.

Thank You, Jesus!

Our heart bubbles over
with joy – we can't hide.
For we're His reflection
because He lives inside.

God's Promise:
The Lord is my strength and shield. I
trust Him with all my heart. He
helps me, and my heart is filled with
joy. I burst out in songs of
thanksgiving.
Psalm 28: 7

Focus:
He fills our heart with joy!

Thank You, Jesus!

The indwelling seal of God's Spirit
is present every minute.
Thank You for this promise –
to all hearts that are repentant.

God's Promise:
Don't you realize that your body is
the temple of the Holy Spirit, who
lives in you and was given to you by
God? You do not belong to yourself.
1 Corinthians 6: 19

Focus:
God's Spirit is with us every
minute.

Thank You, Jesus!

Lord, let Your Holy Spirit
fall afresh on us.
Saturate us with Your Power.
Infill us with Your Love.

God's Promise:
Some of us are Jews, some are
Gentiles, some are slaves, and some
are free. But we have all been
baptized into one body by one Spirit,
and we all share the same Spirit.
1 Corinthians 12: 13

Focus:
Let Your Holy Spirit fall afresh on
us.

Thank You, Jesus!

The fragrance of our Living God
is sweeter than the flowers.
Yet He holds the universe in place
with His might and power.

God's Promise:
He uses us to spread the knowledge
of Christ everywhere, like a sweet
perfume.
2 Corinthians 2: 14b

Focus:
The fragrance of our Living God
Is sweeter than the flowers.

Thank You, Jesus!

God's Holy Spirit lives in us.
We don't have to pray Him down.
In Him, we praise our Father!
We were lost- but now are found.

God's Promise:
You have received the Holy Spirit,
and He lives within you, so you don't
need anyone to teach you what is
true.
1 John 2: 27a

Focus:
The Holy Spirit is our Teacher.

Thank You, Jesus!

In the depths of our spirit,
The Holy Spirit resides –
Giving hope and assurance
That our soul never dies.

God's Promise:
Let all that I am wait quietly before God, for my hope is in Him.
Psalm 62: 5

Focus:
Our hope is in Him.

Thank You, Jesus!

The Holy Spirit grips our heart.
We are never more the same.
His precious Love is from above.
And Jesus is His Name.

God's Promise:
Since we are living by the Spirit, let us follow the Spirit's leading in every part of our lives.
Galations 5: 25

Focus:
The Holy Spirit grips our heart and Jesus is His Name!

Thank You, Jesus!

God placed His Spirit in our heart,
a small deposit of His Love.
This is a gentle foretaste
of our life with Him above.

God's Promise:
He has identified us as His Own by
placing the Holy Spirit in our hearts
as the first installment that
guarantees everything He has
promised us.
2 Corinthians 1: 22

Focus:
The Holy Spirit in our heart is a
gentle foretaste of our heavenly
home.

Thank You, Jesus!

He who lives inside our heart,
is our Advocate and hope.
He guides us in the hard times.
And soothes our aching soul.

God's Promise:
"I will ask the Father, and He will give you another Advocate, who will never leave you.
John 14: 16

Focus:
Our Lord will never leave us.

Thank You, Jesus!

Chapter 7

Eternal Life

Our Lord is sending out a signal.
His time for us has come.
Light has broken in the darkness.
He longs to say to all, "Well done."

God's Promise:
"The Master was full of praise. "Well done, my good and faithful servant."
Matthew 25: 21a

Focus:
We long to hear our Savior say, "Well done."

Thank You, Jesus!

In eternity – our Lord will reign.
There will be no temple in it.
God's Light and the Holy Lamb
will shine wth glory every minute.

God's Promise:
The city has no need of sun or moon,
for the glory of God illuminates the
city, and the Lamb is its Light.
Revelation 21: 23

Focus:
The Lamb will be its Light.

Thank You, Jesus!

When this road ends into another,
another paved in purest gold.
When we behold the face of Jesus,
at last, we'll be made whole.

God's Promise:
The wall was made of jasper, and the
city was pure gold, as clear as glass.
Revelation 21: 18

Focus:
We can only imagine!

Thank You, Jesus!

With open arms, we'll see Him,
returning in all His glory.
Just as He promised in His Word-
The completion of His Love Story.

God's Promise:
When Christ, who is your life, is
revealed to the whole world, you will
share in all His glory.
Colossians 3: 4

Focus:
We will share His glory!

Thank You, Jesus!

Beyond the reach of sin and evil,
inside the gates of pearl.
We'll know joy - only imagined
in God's perfect, heavenly world.

God's Promise:
The twelve gates were made of pearls
– each gate from a single pearl! And
the main street was pure gold, as
clear as glass.
Revelation 21: 12

Focus:
Arm in arm with Jesus, we will walk
through those gates of pearl.

Thank You, Jesus!

We are God's prized possession.
With Jesus – a joint heir.
A permanent place at His table –
For us – He has prepared.

God's Promise:
And the angel said to me, "Write this: Blessed are those who are invited to the wedding feast of the Lamb." And he added, "These are true words that come from God."
Revelation 19: 9

Focus:
We can have a permanent place at our Lord's table.

Thank You, Jesus!

Our Lord – so rich in mercy
surely knows each one by name.
We look forward to our home –
with no sad goodbyes or pain.

God's Promise:
But now, O Jacob, listen to the Lord
who created you.
O Israel, the One who formed you
says: "Do not be afraid, for I have
ransomed you. I have called you by
name. You are Mine."
Isaiah 43: 1

Focus:
Our Lord knows us by name.

Thank You, Jesus!

When our hearts are grieving,
God holds us in His hand.
There will be a sweet reunion,
a homecoming that will never end.

God's Promise:
Then together with them, we who are still alive and remain on the earth will be caught up in the clouds to meet the Lord in the air. Then we will be with the Lord forever.
1 Thessalonians 4: 17

Focus:
One day – there will be a sweet reunion.

Thank You, Jesus!

Eden's Tree of Life is blooming
in God's heavenly Paradise.
Its sweet fragrance will remind us
of God's gift – Eternal Life.

God's Promise:
Anyone with ears to hear must listen
to the Spirit and understand what He
is saying to the churches. To
everyone who is victorious I will give
fruit from the tree of life in the
paradise of God.
Revelation 2: 7

Focus:
We will enjoy the sweet fragrance of
the Tree of Life.

Thank You, Jesus!

Our final glimpse of this life
will reveal our glimpse of Him.
At last we'll see His precious face.
Our Savior – Heaven's Gem.

God's Promise:
And this is the plan: At the right
time He will bring everything together under the authority of Christ
– everything in heaven and on earth.
Ephesians 1: 10

Focus:
We will see His face!

Thank You, Jesus!

John wrote of The New Jerusalem
where there will be no sorrow.
What glorious joy awaits us –
in God's great tomorrow.

God's Promise:
And I saw the Holy City, The New
Jerusalem, coming down from God
out of Heaven like a bride beautifully
dressed for her husband.
Revelation 21: 2

Focus:
What glorious joy awaits us.

Thank You, Jesus!

The many questions that we have
one day – we'll clearly see.
When life becomes eternal life.
Where forever – we will be.

God's Promise:
And this is the way to have eternal
life – to know You, the only true God,
and Jesus Christ, the One You sent to
earth.
John 17: 3

Focus:
Our life will never end.

Thank You, Jesus!

The many joys we share in life
with friends and family dear –
are just a foretaste of the joys
we have waiting over there.

God's Promise:
"Now I am coming to You. I told
them many things while I was with
them in this world so they would be
filled with My joy."
John 17: 13

Focus:
We are filled with the joy that no one
can take away.

Thank You, Jesus!

Our temporary home on earth
is a place of sweet abode.
But our eternal home prepared
is more precious than pure gold.

God's Promise:
For we know that when this earthly
tent we live in is taken down (that is,
when we die and leave this earthly
body), we will have a house in
heaven, an eternal body made for us
by God Himself and not by human
hands.
2 Corinthians 5: 1

Focus:
He is preparing a home not built by
human hands.

Thank You, Jesus!

We've received our invitation.
A banquet table is being spread.
God has prepared a celebration
where all His children may be fed.

God's Promise:
Come to me with your ears wide open. Listen, and you will find life. I will make an everlasting covenant with you. I will give you all the unfailing love I promised to David.
Isaiah 55: 3

Focus:
God's invitation is for all.

Thank You, Jesus!

Worldly things are temporary.
Youthful dreams grow dim.
But when we see Him as He is,
we shall be like Him.

God's Promise:
Dear friends, we are already God's children, but He has not yet shown us what we will be like when Christ appears. But we do know that we will be like Him, for we will see Him as He really is.
1 John 3: 2

Focus:
We will be like Him!

Thank You, Jesus!

"Whoever lives and believes in Me will never, ever die."
We believe Your promise, Lord.
Thank You for eternal life!

God's Promise:
"Everyone who lives in Me and believes in Me will never ever die."
John 11: 26a

Focus:
If we live and believe in Him, we will never die.

Thank You, Jesus!

Little children will be contented.
All abuse and fear will cease.
A lamb and wolf will feed together
in our Lord's new dawn of peace.

God's Promise:
In that day the wolf and the lamb will
live together; the leopard will lie
down with the baby goat. The calf
and the yearling will be safe with the
lion, and a little child will lead them
all.
Isaiah 11: 6

Focus:
We will be safe in God's new dawn of
peace.

Thank You, Jesus!

Blinded eyes will all be opened.
Crippled legs will walk again.
Our thoughts that often wander
will, at last, be free of sin.

God's Promise:
And when He comes, He will open
the eyes of the blind and unplug the
ears of the deaf. The lame will leap
like a deer, and those who cannot
speak will sing for joy! Springs will
gush forth in the wilderness, and
streams will water the wasteland.
Isaiah 35: 5-6

Focus:
In that place, there will be no
handicaps or tears!

Thank You, Jesus!

Broken minds will see clearly.
Broken bodies will be whole.
Our new and heavenly bodies
will replace our sin-sick soul.

God's Promise:
The reward for trusting Him will be
the salvation of your souls.
1 Peter 1: 9

Focus:
We will be perfect – even as He is
perfect.

Thank You, Jesus!

We will hear a shout from heaven!
One day – all sin will cease!
One day – no separation!
One day – forever peace!

God's Promise:
God has ascended with a mighty shout. The Lord has ascended with trumpets blaring.
Psalm 47: 5

Focus:
One day – forever peace.

Thank You, Jesus!

As far as east is from the west,
our Lord has placed our sins.
We will hear Him say, "My child,
In My Kingdom – enter in."

God's Promise:
He has removed our sins as far from
us as the east is from the west.
Psalm 103: 12

Focus:
He has erased all our sins.

Thank You, Jesus!

In the world, He was homeless.
But He spoke of a heavenly home.
It's a longing of our own heart,
when we know Him as our own.

God's Promise:
And we believers also groan, even though we have the Holy Spirit within us as a foretaste of future glory, for we long for our bodies to be released from sin and suffering. We, too, wait with eager hope for the day when God will give us our full rights as His adopted children, including the new bodies He has promised us.
Romans 8: 23

Focus:
He has promised us new bodies.

Thank You, Jesus!

We're always kind of homesick
for the home we've never seen.
It's a joyful kind of longing
for all of God's redeemed.

God's Promise:
"I will comfort you there in Jerusalem as a mother comforts her child.
Isaiah 66: 13

Focus:
We have a joyful kind of longing to be with our Lord and our loved ones.

Thank You, Jesus!

We are God's uncut jewels,
that He is polishing with grace.
He is molding us for heaven,
where we shall behold His face.

God's Promise:
Let us come boldly to the throne of
our gracious God. There we will
receive His mercy, and we will find
grace to help us when we need it
most.
Hebrews: 4: 16

Focus:
Our Lord is polishing us with grace.

Thank You, Jesus!

On earth our sight is clouded.
We can only see so much.
When the veil is lifted,
we will feel His loving touch.

God's Promise:
Whenever someone turns to the
Lord, the veil is taken away.
2 Corinthians 3: 16

Focus:
One day, we will clearly see and
understand.

Thank You, Jesus!

Life is a beautiful journey
where great memories are shared.
But it's not our destination.
So much more has been prepared.

God's Promise:
"For I know the plans I have for you," says the Lord. "They are plans for good and not for disaster, to give you a future and a hope."
Jeremiah 29: 11

Focus:
Our Lord has great plans for each of us.

Thank You, Jesus!

We have a hunger for heaven.
Worldly things are not our own.
Our heart is centered on God's will
with sights on our heavenly home.

God's Promise:
Think about the things of heaven,
not the things of earth.
Colossians 2: 9

Focus:
Lord, keep our thoughts centered on
things above.

Thank You, Jesus!

No eye has seen a greater wonder.
No ear has heard a sweeter song.
No mind imagined all the joy
prepared for us in our new home.

God's Promise:
That is what the Scriptures mean when they say, "No eye has seen, no ear has heard, and no mind has imagined what God has prepared for those who love Him.
1 Corinthians 2: 9

Focus:
We can only imagine what our Lord has prepared for us.

Thank You, Jesus!

Just as surely as He came,
He is coming back again.
Every tongue will call Him Lord.
And every knee will bow to Him.

God's Promise:
And every tongue declare that Jesus
Christ is Lord, to the glory of God the
Father.
Philippians 2: 11

Focus:
Every tongue will declare Him Lord!

Thank You, Jesus!

If our name is written in heaven,
we have reason to rejoice.
His blessings are all around us,
when we make Him our choice.

God's Promise:
All who are victorious will inherit all these blessings, and I will be their God, and they will be my children.
Revelation 21: 7

Focus:
If our name is written in heaven, we have reason to rejoice.

Thank You, Jesus!

God Himself is waiting there
with power to transform us.
With opens arms He welcomes us
where nothing more can harm us.

God's Promise:
When our dying bodies have been transformed into bodies that will never die, this Scripture will be fulfilled: "Death is swallowed up in victory."
1 Corinthians 15: 54

Focus:
Death is swallowed up in victory!

Thank You, Jesus!

There is a place, a wonderful place
that Jesus is preparing.
It's purchased with His precious
blood –
and nurtured with His caring.

God's Promise:
"There is more than enough room in
My Father's home. If this were not
so, would I have told you that I am
going to prepare a place for you?"
John 14: 2

Focus:
Our Lord has especially prepared a
place for us.

Thank You, Jesus!

Three things will last forever.
It's God's promise from above.
When worldly things crumble,
we have faith, and hope, and love.

God's Promise:
Three things will last forever – faith,
hope, and love – and the greatest of
these is love.
1 Corinthians 13: 13

Focus:
Love will last forever.

Thank You, Jesus!

When we walk into Paradise,
and we're bathed in purest love –
we will fall to our knees in worship
of our Savior from above.

God's Promise:
When I think of all this, I fall to my knees and pray to the Father, the Creator of everything in heaven and on earth.
Ephesians 3: 14-15

Focus:
We will fall to our knees in praise.

Thank You, Jesus!

No asphalt in that city.
The streets – with gold – are laid.
The tree of life is blooming.
The fragrant blooms will never fade.

God's Promise:
The main street was pure gold, as clear as glass.
Revelation 21: 21a

Focus:
We will walk on streets of gold.

Thank You, Jesus!

Eternal joy comes in the morning!
Our struggles last but for a day.
If compared with Heaven's glory,
earthly troubles quickly fade.

God's Promise:
Weeping may last through the night,
but joy comes in the morning.
Psalm 30: 5b

Focus:
Joy comes in the morning.

Thank You, Jesus!

An inheritance incorruptible –
In heaven – reserved for us.
It is our hope when we accept
His grace and endless Love.

God's Promise:
We have a priceless inheritance – an
inheritance that is kept in heaven for
you, pure and undefiled, beyond the
reach of change and decay.
1 Peter 1: 4

Focus:
We have an inheritance with Jesus
when we give Him our heart.

Thank You, Jesus!

In eternity – our Lord will reign;
there will be no temple in it.
God's Light and the Holy Lamb
shines with glory every minute.

God's Promise:
The city has no need of sun or moon,
for the glory of God illuminates the
city, and the Lamb is its light.
Revelation 21: 23

Focus:
Our Lord will shine on us forever.

Thank You, Jesus!

Jesus said, "I am going
to prepare a place for you."
We believe His precious promise.
His Word is ever true.

God's Promise:
"Soon the world will no longer see
Me, but you will see Me. Since I live,
you also will live.
John 14: 19

Focus:
Because He lives, we too shall live.

Thank You, Jesus!

God's promise of heaven
is an anchor for our soul.
Firm and secure, we rest assured
He is our eternal hope.

God's Promise:
This hope is a strong and trust-worthy anchor for our souls. It leads us through the curtain into God's inner sanctuary.
Hebrews 6: 19

Focus:
God is an anchor for our soul.

Thank You, Jesus!

Lord, as we look around us,
we see much pain and sorrow.
May we ever see before us –
Your promise of tomorrow.

God's Promise:
Think about the things of heaven,
not the things of earth.
Colossians 3: 2

Focus:
He has promised us a bright tomorrow with Him.

Thank You, Jesus!

Bodies of dust are temporary.
We are here for just a while.
Our reborn spirit is eternal.
We'll look upon His loving smile.

God's Promise:
We are God's masterpiece. He has created us anew in Christ Jesus, so we can do the good things He planned for us long ago.
Ephesians 2: 10

Focus:
Our bodies of dust are temporary. Our new bodies will be eternal.

Thank You, Jesus!

It is hard to imagine
a world with no sin.
But that's what we're promised
when our Lord comes again.

God's Promise:
I have written this to you who believe in the Name of the Son of God,
so that you may know you have
eternal life.
Ephesians 2: 10

Focus:
We can know we have eternal life.

Thank You, Jesus!

Christ in us – our hope of glory!
You have given life to us!
This will ever be our story!
We praise You for eternal love!

God's Promise:
This is the secret: Christ lives in you.
This gives you assurance of sharing
His glory.
Colossians 1: 27b

Focus:
Christ is our hope of glory!

Thank You, Jesus!

God promised a New Jerusalem!
He will reign on a purified earth!
With eternal joy, we'll praise Him.
No fears! No tears! No hurt!

God's Promise:
I saw the holy city, the New Jerusalem, coming down from God out of heaven like a bride beautifully dressed for her husband.
Revelation 21: 2

Focus:
God promised a New Jerusalem.

Thank You, Jesus!

"Don't store up treasures here on earth, where moths eat them and rust destroys them, and where thieves break in and steal. Store your treasures in heaven, where moths and rust cannot destoy, and thieves do not break in and steal. Wherever your treasure is, there the desires of your heart will also be."

Matthew 6: 19-21

Other books by Lillie Rhodes Manley

God Loves You and Me: They will be delighted as well as educated through Scriptures that teach them that though God controls the universe, He loves you and me. *Treasureify.com*

A Picnic With Jesus: A Picnic With Jesus is a Bible Story Book for Children that will bring joy to the heart of every child and adult who reads it. The living color prints will grab the attention of younger children as they hang on every word of this beautiful kid's Bible Story book that is filled with happiness and adventure.

A Christmas Light: What is that light – way up in the sky? Is that a star – shining down so bright? These questions and more will be asked by children of all ages.

Sweet Whispers of Hope: You are invited to join Lillie Rhodes Manley on her own tear-filled journey of faith as she learned to listen to Sweet Whispers of

Hope from the God she has walked with since childhood. Treasureify.com

ONE LAST THING

If you enjoyed this book or found it useful I'd be very grateful if you'd post a short review on Amazon. Your support really does make a difference and I read all the reviews personally so I can get your feedback and make this book even better.

If you'd like to leave a review then all you need to do is click the review link on this book's page on Amazon here:

`Treasurefy.com/`
`ReviewThievesCantSteal`

Thanks again for your support!

GOD PROMISED A NEW JERUSALEM

Notes

GOD PROMISED A NEW JERUSALEM

Notes